Dear Reader,

*   **Places Within My Heart** *evolved around journals I kept during a visit to Egypt in 1984 and is the embryo of my memoir* **Behind The Magic Mirror** *published in 2002.*

During the trip back home from Egypt and Israel and then back to New Jersey, I remember very little of importance that transpired during those days coming back to reality. My mind was occupied with new discoveries about myself and with the new interest I had in searching for the truth as to what had happened in the disappearance of my ex-husband, Jennings, who suffered from schizophrenia.

I wanted to be able to finally close that chapter in my life. I had a beginning and a middle and I would not stop until I had an end. I wanted an answer for all of us. I wanted an end for all of us. A final closure, so that we could go on with our lives.

In 1995, fifteen years after Jennings' disappearance and ten years after my journey to Egypt, I finally was at the end of my painful odyssey. Piece by piece I put

*together the puzzle of what happened in my late husband's life. Those last months and days, down to the final hour of his life that I chronicled in **Behind The Magic Mirror**. Each new lead opened up to me information about a man, a personality that I did not know. A life that joined to me was also very much indeed foreign to me.*

I now would like to share with you the journey down the Nile that allowed me to find myself and face my need for closure.

Sandra Hart

Places Within My Heart

Cover Art by Brett Thompson
copyright©2006, Myartisansway Press
Cover photo Sandra Hart

Library of Congress Control Number: 2002110097
ISBN 0-9715525-1-7

Published by
Myartisansway Press
10 Ballinswood Road Suite 3
Atlantic Highlands, New Jersey 07716
www.sandrahart.net

Printed in the United States of America
Published in 2006

Places Within My Heart

Places Within My Heart

BY SANDRA HART

Behind The Magic Mirror
Death Certificate
Behind The Magic Mirror Revised Parts I and II
Tit ForTat, This and That
Marshell's Surprise
Lucy Line

Places Within My Heart

Places Within My Heart

My Journey Along the River of Life

Sandra Hart

Ballinswood Books   New York • New Jersey

Places Within My Heart

For my family and friends
With Love

Places Within My Heart

To my readers
Forgive the mistakes that are always there

Places Within My Heart

CHAPTERS

The River of Life
Beginnings
Luxor
Hatshepsut
Oasis
The Story Elizabeth
Saying Goodbye
Fathama

Places Within My Heart

Betwixt and Between

When I was a child I could see
A plane of un-scaled mountains
Beckoning, challenging me.

Then as time went by
Clearer became the mountains
But dimmer the way.

In the winter of my seasons
And wiser, they say
A latent thought dwells.

Were the obstacles as steep
As my uncertain brows did see
And the paths so narrow?

Or the limitations, perhaps,
Within me.

Sandra Hart

Places Within My Heart

In 1984 we were the first group of Western tourists entering through Jordan from Israel traveling to Egypt under the then new agreement to allow tourism from Israel to Egypt.

We found the Egyptians to be very hospitable throughout the country and in 1984, very pro-America. Our journey down the Nile, indeed, proved to be very amazing and one that I shall never forget.

Places Within My Heart

Prologue

For those of you who have read my memoir, **Behind The Magic Mirror,** you are familiar with the story of my life up to and until the year 2002.

I grew up in Steubenville, a gloomy Ohio valley steel town on the banks of the Ohio River and as a young woman realized my dream of leaving the industrial grime and smoke that I grew to hate.

Attending college far away from home was not only a way out, but also during my years at school, life afforded me a break. I was asked to audition for Bert Claster, the creator of a popular children's television show, Romper Room, syndicated throughout the world.   This occurrence changed my life forever and I began on a whirlwind of life-changing events that caused me to eventually lead a double life. My public persona was that of a successful anchor woman, but my private life was one of personal pain and constant terror.

It took me years to realize that I had suppressed so much of the searing times with my schizophrenic ex-husband. It was not until my trip to Egypt that I was able to start mourning my past and to begin understanding that I had to have answers. This was the only way I could completely exorcise the demons in my past and have some type of closure.

It took me eleven years to sort out the mystery of my husband's disappearance and to also sort out my feelings when I discovered the truth.

When the ball dropped in New York's Times Square on the Millennium and we all survived while entering the next century, I knew I couldn't put it off any longer. I had to tell my story.

My initial plan was to combine a journal that I kept traveling the Nile River in 1984 with the story of my life and the investigation I started thereafter involving Jennings' whereabouts. I had planned to use my journal and, in flashbacks, tell the rest of the story.

In the end, I felt the manuscript was not easy to follow, so I finally wound up writing three different books that covered various aspects of my life and the true crime mystery revolving around my ex-husband.

I had forgotten all about my travel journal until I recently bought a new file cabinet. While I was busily going through and exchanging the files, I came across the worn pages of my journal telling my thoughts about our 1984 trip. I flipped through the first pages, deciding whether or not it was a 'keeper'. I found myself instantly becoming so immersed in the content of my writings, that my cleaning stopped.

Arthur and I had just come back from a world cruise and Egypt had two ports on our itinerary. The trip and Egypt still very fresh in my mind, I read on.

I found the earlier entries detailing my thoughts and impressions as I traveled along the Nile had started to awaken within me fond memories of our first visit there.

I wasn't too sure that anyone but me would be interested in my emotional evolution during that prior journey to Egypt, so I gave my journal to several of my family and good friends to read.

They, in turn, unanimously gave me the encouragement I needed to go forward with this manuscript, even though I assured them it would be a small book. I did not want to dilute the importance of my journey with anything but those events that truly loosened my wings and shaped my desire to return home and put all of the pieces of my past together.

I hope you will enjoy traveling with me on my journey along the River of Life.

Conundrum

What words plea
Upon the page
To tell my tale
Expose my soul
So I can feel
So you can see
What I know?
Me.

Sandra Hart

I've known rivers;
I've known rivers ancient as the world and older
Than the flow of human blood in human veins.
My soul has grown deep like the rivers.
—Langston Hughes—

The River of Life

Clickety-click. Clickety-click. The sounds of the train's wheels came steady and even; a metronome marking the beats of a song. To-

and-fro, to-and-fro, to-and-fro. The inertia of the movement gently rocked our bodies to its rhythm. Our compartment with its worn cloth seats was the first comfortable place we had been since we left Israel and I stretched my legs to capture the cool air flowing beneath my calves. We had started early the day before motoring from Tel Aviv through Taba, crossed the Sinai to the Gulf of Suez and headed north to the canal where we crossed and continued west into Cairo. There we boarded the train for our long journey down the Nile.

Yesterday's travel had been through miles of echoing desert silence. Harsh and rocky surfaces bleached dry by thousands of years of baking sun flanked either side of the road that sliced through the desert's breast. Little evidence of life was visible except for an occasional Bedouin tent encampment far beyond the road's edge. Now, as we headed west it was as though we had entered another world. Here near the river's edge and beyond as far as the eye could see the land became green and life began again.

Outside my sand-spattered train window the landscape and the life on it mirrored a time long past. Low palm-roofed houses, abandoned tractors rusting in the fields next to donkeys hitched with primitive plows. Modern technology abandoned for more familiar methods of working the fertile soil along the river.

Groups of women scrubbed the family wash on large rocks while naked babies slept nearby in baskets and children skipped stones that skimmed creating small uneven hiccups on the surface of their murky playground. Mile upon mile, I watched them launder, bathe, play and drink from its waters- this river of life. The Nile.

It's like looking through The National Geographic, I thought, remembering when my brother and I as children would spend hours poring over its colorful pictures. In our imaginations with each turn of the page we traveled to strange exotic places we had never before seen. Only now, I was here and the reality of what I was witnessing was almost overwhelming, enveloped safely in my coach behind my window, trespassing, unnoticed, into the lives of a culture, familiar, yet so foreign to me.

My husband and I had spent great time preparing for this trip. Gathering brochures, scouring travelogues for information that would make our vacation run smoothly. Initially, we had just planned on visiting his relatives in Israel, spending the bulk of our time traveling and covering much of the historical sights, but the more we researched, the more convinced we were to include Egypt on our itinerary.

Arthur had never been to Israel before and was looking forward to seeing his relatives and praying at the Wailing Wall in Jerusalem. I was realizing a life-long dream of visiting the sights where Jesus was supposed to have performed miracles. Our diverse religions and heritages, Judaic and Christian, would come together again as it had in our marriage. And now, here we were in Egypt, the second leg of our journey, traveling along the Nile by train.

I looked over at my husband sleeping soundly with his head facing away from the window's light, his jaw slack and moving ever so slightly in cadence with his breathing. My son had gone to the club car to get our itinerary from the tour guide, his backpack was open and thrown carelessly across his empty seat. Just like a boy, I thought.

I suppose his father's disappearance when he

was still so young has made it twice as hard for me to realize that he is growing up. Hard for me to let go. I'm so used to doing it all alone most of the time. Habit really is my worst competitor. Sometimes I feel like an octopus with tentacles stretched everywhere. Arthur was never married before and never had any children, but he has done well, considering. But *I'm* still learning, even at this point.

"What?" Arthur said half asleep.

"Nothing Dear, I was talking to myself again. Go back to sleep."

"What time is it?"

"Early," I replied.

He closed his eyes, adjusted his sleeping position and his jaw ever so slightly dropped again. He was asleep.

I watched him and marveled at how he could sleep so easily. I was never able to sleep on anything moving. I don't know why, but ever since I was a child it was so.

My, how being here brings back memories of my childhood. I hadn't been on a train in years. I remember during the war we lived in Washington, D.C. and traveled by train to my grandparents' home in Ohio. My father would

29

always book a drawing room which consisted of several bunk beds and a lavatory. I would play games on the floor in the center of the room. When bedtime came, my father must have read me hours of stories trying to get me to sleep on those overnight trips westward through the Allegheny Mountains. Daddy would hold me on his lap and sing to me. I remember resting my head on his shirt and hearing the deep resonance of his voice through his chest. It was that soothing resonance that finally brought the Sandman.

I looked at my watch. Seven-thirty. I could let Arthur sleep a little longer, at least until Lee returns. I studied his handsome face, peaceful and relaxed. His fair skin had been tanned by the hot Israeli sun and accentuated the whiteness of his fine wavy hair. He really must have been so handsome when he was young, I thought...with those blue eyes.

I turned toward the window and the passing landscape along the Nile wondering what powerful secrets and stories its waters held.

God knows *I* was no stranger to secrets.

It was the discovery in my parent's attic when I was fifteen that revealed more secrets than I was prepared to find in a lifetime. Three yellowed newspaper clippings under the filmy 20's flapper dress I someday dreamed to wear. In Mother's trunk one clipping was an announcement of the debut of a young woman. I studied the picture of the girl . She was big-boned and had dark hair and by now must have been at least twenty years older than I. Under the picture I read the name of my father as her father and other names of her mother and step-father that I had never even heard of. None of these people; the plain girl, the mother, the step-father. None.

The other two were marriage announcements of my mother to some stranger and the other was her divorce announcement from the same stranger.

I never confronted my parents with my discovery, since I wasn't supposed to be snooping in the trunk, anyway. And that was that. So it evolved and our cycle began. Their secrets became my secrets. To this day, I don't know why my parents chose not to share their earlier lives with me. I imagine what other secrets they have about their lives will go with them to their graves like the muddy currents stirring in the bottom of the Nile.

The past is but the beginning of a beginning
And all that is and has been
Is but the twilight of the dawn.
—*Herbert George Wills*—

Beginnings

"Mom," Lee popped his head in through the doorway, "they're serving breakfast up front, should I get a table?"

"Okay. I'll wake Arthur and freshen up. Be there in five minutes."

"Where do you want to sit?" he asked.

"Anywhere. It doesn't matter. Maybe close to where we were last night. That was a good spot."

"Okay," he replied and flashed a boyish grin my way before he closed the door.

I splashed cold water on my face from the small basin in our compartment and ran a comb through my hair. Lipstick would have to wait, I thought. It was too hot. It would have to do.

"Arthur. Arthur. You'd better wake up. Breakfast." I knew the mention of food would sink into his brain and quickly bring him out of the deepest unconscious state. It had always worked before. Food is his elixir of life. His lean six-foot frame was a testimony to his ability to devour an enormous amount of food and not gain a pound.

I gently touched his shoulder. He stirred and opened his eyes.

"Breakfast, " I said, "Lee's holding a table for us in the dining car."

Arthur stretched and moved his hand to grasp mine resting on his shoulder.

"Stop that! We're not exactly alone you know. Look out there. The world is watching us."

"All the better my dear, said the big bad wolf."

I bent down and kissed his moist forehead. "Get up, Lover Boy, let's eat. You've got my rain check, okay. We'll be in a hotel tonight."

"You're no fun anymore," he pouted. "Remember…" he teased raising his eyebrow in his best Gable imitation. "Who needs to eat?"

"Sorry. When I'm hungry I lose my head…my priorities get confused. In case you've forgotten, I'm hypoglycemic. Now get up, splash some water on your face and put out your fire. Lee's waiting and probably half-starved by now. Besides we're to arrive in Luxor at nine, that doesn't give us much time."

We left our compartment and made our way down the train's narrow corridor, passing rows of numbered cabin doors until we reached the dining car.

Relationships. Do they always evolve into something either so comfortable, or uncomfortable, that it becomes platonic? From the initial stages of passion to the point, finally, where you know your partner's thoughts before they even speak.

Not that it can be a bad thing for some. There is a certain comfort in knowing. But maybe marriage and living together kills the mystery, no surprises anymore. The way he squeezes the toothpaste. How he dominates the remote on the television and reads every label when shopping for food. Little things become big things. The dynamics change. The reality of what we now know about each other after all these years, the trying imperfections that become magnified, it's hard to light a match with that. I wondered if it happens to everyone, or is it just to dented cans like Arthur and me.

Arthur grew up in the poorest part of the East Bronx in New York with an impoverished, frustrated, religious mother and meek father who were immigrants. Screaming was the way things were handled in his household. He never had a toy and play was a game of stickball in the streets. On hot evenings they took their blankets and pillows and slept in Crotona Park with hundreds of other sweltering people. During the leanest of times, he and his gentle father sold peanuts in that same park.

I, on the other hand, came from a wealthy family whose ancestors set foot in America generations ago. My father started drinking heavily right after I was born and except for a few fine pieces of furniture, lost it all. We landed at my mother's parents' farm in Ohio with suitcases in hand after World War II. When Daddy came home full of whiskey, there was plenty of screaming in my house, too. He stopped drinking when I was about twelve, but the footprints were already deeply imprinted on my sensitive soul.

Our breakfast coffee was served in small cups, but the size and the intensity was deceiving. The thick, dark brew, stronger than espresso, for me, had to be weakened with lots of warm milk from the heavy metal creamer. We ate from the basket of assorted biscuits and figs on the table. The former leaving tiny crumbs around our plates. I resisted the urge to scoop them away in the cup of my hand as I had so often done at our family table at home. Instead, I concentrated on the thick black brew dancing dangerously to the edge of my cup with each movement of the train and wondered whether it was wise to add any more milk to it. Gravity made up my mind for me. As the train lurched on, part of the syrupy liquid escaped over the lip of the cup and spilled onto the crisp white linen cloth that covered the table. A spreading muddy puddle impregnated the loose crumbs in its path and blew them up into moist bits of dough. So much for esthetics, I thought, as the coffee made a river of its own and slowly absorbed into the linen.

The boys were in animated conversation, going over the maps of Luxor and the day's itinerary. How lucky I should feel having found Arthur just when my son was at the age of really needing a father. I observed Master Scout and son carefully laying out the day on the trail. What other man would have been sane enough, or possibly crazy enough, to take on a wife with three children already attached firmly to her bosom. Especially in the prime of his bachelor life, never having had experienced the trials of married life before, or having to be responsible for anyone but himself, let alone a ready-made family.

Sometimes I wish I could give him more, not to deprive him of what he thought marriage would be. But having been widowed so early in life and managing on my own for so long has made me different than I would have been had we met years earlier. I'm used to caring for myself. Arthur, too, was independent until late in life, so unfortunately for both of us, there will always be a part of each of us that we cannot share with anyone. Not even each other.

Mother would tell me stories of my running up onto the stage in the movies when I was a child. I would struggle free of her arms and run up the aisle just to be a part of the wonderful life that was on the screen.

Well, I thought glancing over at Arthur, this is not the movies. I am what I am, he is what he is and our life together is what it is. That script I can't change.

I can't change the past. For Arthur. For me. For my children. I wonder if they were given a chance to start over with someone else if they would choose it? Crawl back into the womb and arrive into a more perfect life. I quickly dismissed this bizarre thought as the train droned on toward our destination and I watched the two men in my life plan our first day in Luxor.

The Desert

Nameless surgeons cut the paper-edged road
exposing
> Her soul.

Ancient majestic arms rise from the sands
stretched toward
> Her God.

Tears slide silently from her eyes and fall liquid
pools of
> Her pain.

Travelers we come along that surgeon's mark
between
> Her breasts.

Trespassing   each shadow, each sunset, we
wonder at
> Her Beauty.

Her life becomes a part of us and we inhale the
powers of
> Her spirit.

Sandra Hart

I will not mourn, although my heart is torn,
Oh, love forever lost!
I will not mourn.
—Heinrich Heine—

Luxor

In spite of the large fan circulating far above our heads on the ceiling, the lobby in our hotel at Luxor was only a few degrees cooler than the desert heat outside. As I looked around, I would not have been surprised to see Humphry Bogart sitting at the bar while the polished mahogany piano with yellowed ivories in the corner of the room twanged out soulful tunes.

I was brought back to reality by the sight of a

tall Nubian porter dressed in a galabiyya. His long, sinewy body moved gracefully toward us and his face displayed no greeting until he reached us.

"Bags, Mam'. How many?"

Before we could reply, his strong arms scooped up our luggage.

"Follow me. Nice room, end of hall, just right for you, Mam'."

His head turned back our way and he flashed a leathery grin as he darted away with us double-stepping to keep up with his long-legged strides.

"Would I love to have him on our track team," Lee whispered as he jogged along side of me. I jerked his sleeve as a signal to end that conversation for fear his not-too-silent whispers could be heard by our Nubian escort.

He lead us down the long dark hallway and stopped just right off the corridor to a door marked with a brass number '8'. The unlocked door swung open to reveal a large open space with floor to ceiling windows on the far side. Tall dark green louvers opened on either side, letting in the hot morning sun. A double bed and chair were on the right and the left wall had a doorway that lead into a smaller room that was to serve as Lee's space while we were here. The high ceiling had the familiar fans like those in the lobby and were slowly moving the stale air about the room.

I tilted my face toward the fans to catch the slight swirling of air and my eyes caught something dark on the ceiling. I slid my sunglasses down on the edge of my nose to get a clearer view.

"Look. Up there," I squealed.

Arthur and Lee craned their necks upwards.

"Neat." Lee affirmed. "They're moving up there alright. Wow. What are they?"

"Not to worry, Mam', they're harmless. They will not come down to bother you," the Nubian said as he motioned upward toward the ceiling.

"We don't have these at home," Lee replied, obviously delighted at this new celestial discovery.

Our friend didn't even glance upward, "Just little lizards up there. They will come and go and not bother you down here. They not looking to eat you," he said with a slight chuckle. "Less bugs to eat on you. They have big appetite."

I wasn't too sure I believed him, but his cool

English manner was somewhat convincing.

Arthur crossed his generous palm with a few American coins and he was gone, his long garment brushing against his legs as he moved toward the door and out of the room.

Lee took his bag and went to check out his quarters and I walked over to the tall window near the bed. The view was rather surreal. Lush thick grass grew on the ground below our room and in the center I could see a small pool half-filled with dark water; algae clinging to the edges where the water met the cracked sides of the cement pond. Neglect and the desert heat had obviously taken its toll on this tiny oasis in the unkempt gardens. I imagined that in its prime the gardens and vista below must have been meticulously manicured and loved as the English do. I envisioned lovely ladies in broad hats with delicate fans and flowing white linens floating around the grounds on the arms of their distinguished gentlemen.

Time and disregard have ravaged it so, I thought. Now this hotel was only a stop for tourists on their way through to somewhere else. No one who cares enough to stop and stay to appreciate the fading beauty below. How sad.

I felt a soft kiss on the side of my neck as Arthur slid his hands around my waist.

"What are you thinking about over here? You're so quiet."

"I don't know. I guess how painful it is to grow old. Why can't we find a perfect point in our lives and just stay there forever."

"What if my perfect point is different from your perfect point? We would be frozen in time away from each other. Never to meet. Never to know that what a perfect point it could have been."

"Oh, why are you always so logical!"

"It's just one of the great points about me," he said kissing the other side of my neck. "I'm ready to cash your rain check."

"Your timing is off. My perfect point. Lee probably will pop his head in here any minute now. He has already finished capturing several of those creatures from the ceiling and is about to burst in here with his conquest. I know him. It's been too quiet in there.

No sooner than the words escaped my mouth Lee came vaulting through the door holding a paper sack.

"Dad, I got 'em. Look, two of 'em. I killed a fly

and put it on the window sill and ...zonk! Down they came for lunch. I popped a glass over them 1-2-3."

"Lee, get those things out of here," I cried. "They might be poisonous."

"No way," he responded while carefully holding his prize catch.

"Your Mother's right, Son. Great catch, but you should let them go. Unless our lunch menu isn't so great, then we can have them for dessert."

"Ah, Arthur," he moaned, "do I have to?"

"Afraid so. Take them out and let them go where they want. On second thought, I'll come with you. You're too pleased with yourself to be trusted. We'll find a safe place for them in the garden."

I walked back to the window after they left. Somehow the scene below drew me again to its fantasy. There was a certain mysterious beauty to the decay of what was once grand. Bedsides, I always loved the dramatics of what I imagined transpired in places before our paths crossed. My father always said I thought too much. I can't say now that I disagree with him because it seems that I always create my own drama. Even when it doesn't exist.

I can't remember how long I had been standing there, but after a time a wave of sadness began to envelope me. My body shuttered and an overwhelming feeling of loneliness reached down into the deepest pocket of my soul. The years of un-cried tears welled, spilling uncontrollably from my eyes and streamed down my face. Who would have thought my life would be this. As a child I had such innocent and positive dreams for what I thought was my true destiny. Who would have guessed it wouldn't be like in the movies on the screen I yearned to be behind long ago.

In that room in Luxor, Egypt, a place far away from my home, far away from my roots, my life and memories I had repressed for ten painful years came flooding to the surface.
For some bizarre reason, in that room I felt I could begin to release and morn my past.

I had my plan and God had his. My plan for my life had been cast aside. It didn't matter. For the first time in years I knew I would be okay. Finally, I understood and accepted. Finally I could forgive God. And I could cry.

How sharper than a serpent's tooth it is
To have a thankless child!
—Shakespeare—

Hatshepsut

"Mother…Mother…"

Lee's voice drew me back into the room. I had lost all sense of time and didn't realize how long I had been standing there. I wiped my hand across my face to hide my tears from my son, but they must have dried long ago. My skin felt tight where the salty streams had passed along my cheeks. Something in the room, something outside in that garden, what ever it was, moved me to begin to release and remember a part of my life that had been buried deep within me for a long time. The wound that had been festering

49

finally opened and was regurgitating painful memories and emotions that I thought I had successfully suppressed.

"Mother…are you coming! Hurry up. This place is so neat. You can look across the water and see temples and pyramids. That crazy Dr. Brown forgot his passport on the train and they are taking him back to the American Embassy in Cairo. Dad thinks he must have Alzheimer's disease."

I turned to face him, "You know, Lee, you are a wonder. I don't think I've ever met anyone who can say three whole sentences about three different things without even taking a breath. But it is sad about Dr. Brown. He's been forgetting things this whole trip. I hate to think it, but maybe he *is* suffering from a touch of dementia. I wondered how long he could stay with our tour. And he does seem confused sometimes. Maybe it's the best thing. He'll be in good hands there."

"Come on, Dad's downstairs. The tour bus is going to take us to some ancient ruins and King Tut's tomb. Do we have enough water to take with us. The guide says it will be hot out there."

"Yes, I think so. I'll take this bottled

water…and grab your hat. The sun is strong."

As I turned to leave, I knew I would never forget this room and the faded garden below. I felt as though a heavy weight was lifting from me. I was free to walk forward. I closed the door on my past memories and followed my son down the hall to the waiting bus.

Our tour bus headed first along the east bank of the Nile to the Temple of Luxor just a few kilometers up the road from our hotel. Oham, our guide, explained to us that until the end of the nineteenth century, when excavations began, almost all of Luxor village stood within and on top of an enormous debris-filled temple. Ramses II came along and built six great statues of himself in grand scale that were placed around the courtyard. By his side in knee-high proportions, his wife, Nefertari, stands. Male chauvinism started very early in this culture, I thought. Even though a queen, she was probably lucky to even be immortalized.

My observation was fortified as I entered the grand colonnade. On the wall at the right were reliefs illustrating the Opet festival, an annual fertility rite, during which Amun sailed from nearby Karnak for a love-in with his wife, Mur, who inhabited the temple with their son Khonsu. Then along came Alexander the Great and he had an inner chamber built there with a relief on the outside wall facing the Nile capturing his pharaonic-like pose offering gifts to Amun who is in a state of quite obvious festive erection. Amazing, I mused. Time has changed very little.

The sun was beginning to bear down on us as we again boarded our bus for the Valley of the Kings where we were to see King Tutankhamun's tomb and nearby Hatshepsut's mortuary temple. I had drunk most of my water and was grateful that I had brought along extra bottles of water from the hotel. My arms were burning from the heat of the sun and Lee's red nose had to be attended to with a generous layer of zinc oxide.

Oham handed out box lunches containing flat bread and tamaiya, which is made from fava beans and fried in oil, an orange and Coca-Cola. The heat had taken away my appetite, so I had no trouble sharing my tamaiya with Lee. He was a teenager and recently seemed to have a never-ending quest for food. If I could fill him with enough water and tamaiya until we returned to the hotel for dinner maybe he wouldn't notice the absence of junk food.

After lunch we headed to the West Bank across from Luxor at the north end of the necropolis about six kilometers from the river. As we neared Hatshepsut's Mortuary Temple it seemed to rise out of the desert plain at the foot of a great red mountain of rock. A wide-wedge shaped ramp lead up to what had been three terraces each linked by like ramps. Where there was a garden with fountains and trees thousands of years ago, now only dry open spaces remained.

The story of Hatshepsut is a notable one. During her twenty year rule she lead armies and trade exhibitions, and built one of the greatest monuments in Egypt. She wore a fake beard and switched her appearance from female to male in order to rule as pharaoh in a fundamentally patriarchal society.

As a woman pharaoh, Hatshepsut strongly underlined the legitimacy of the rule with extraordinary reliefs along the Birth Colonnade to our right at the rear of the Middle Terrace showing her divine heritage. I marveled at her wisdom and fortitude in ensuring her immortality in stone. Following her death her step-son resentfully defaced her images on the pillars of the Birth Colonnade. Naturally, he preserved his own. Another ungrateful child. My how history does repeat itself, I thought.

As I left Hatshepsut's mortuary, I turned to look once more at her defaced image on one of the pillars near me. She had been a woman ruling in a male-dominated society. A woman and a mother who's fate cast her to rule, and though challenged all the way to her death by her step-son, she won. In spite if it all, she remains.

In some strange way, I felt a kinship with her spirit. She didn't let the bastards get her down. I would like to have been able to tell her we women are still struggling, having been chosen to bear the fruit of mankind. We are still the benefactors of its pain and pleasures. Only we carry each new generation to term in our wombs. Hatshepsut, we still are the nurturers. We still shape the face of the nations. We still...

Backward turn, Oh Time, in your flight,
Make me a child again just for tonight.
—Elizabeth Akers Allen—

Oasis

The steeply rising road climbed toward the Valley of the Kings and the August heat from the sand around us became almost unbearable as our bus driver shifted his heavy load into second gear and the bus groaned around the northern edge of the Theban Necropolis to our destination.

As we climbed down from the bus, the air was

so heavy it was as though we were stepping into the mouth of a great furnace. The heat grew more intense as we headed for the tomb area. Arthur had reloaded his camera with a new roll of film while on the bus and the three of us entered the guarded area near King Tutankhamun's tomb. Lee went ahead of us and disappeared through the entrance with the other travelers. Arthur was right behind him and I stepped inside the entrance when Arthur turned and called out, "Stay right there. I'll get a great picture if you just stand there in the doorway with the light framing you."

I heard the click of the shutter echo in the silence of the tomb. In an instant we were surrounded by guards, shouting and waving their hands wildly. They reached for Arthur's camera, snatched it away from him and walked back to the guard area shaking their hands and continuing to admonish in Arabic.

"What did I do?" Arthur was in a panic. His camera was his prized possession.

"I don't know. I guess you're not to take pictures here, or something. I didn't see any signs, did you?" I turned and saw Oham talking to the guards. He had stayed on the bus and heard the commotion.

All I could see from my vantage point inside the mouth of the tomb were shaking heads and arms pointing our way. Finally, Oham walked toward us, Arthur's camera in his hand.

"I'm going to hold this until you get back on the bus. Inside the tomb is considered a sacred site and no photographs are allowed on sacred holidays. Sorry."

Arthur pleaded ignorance, but I know secretly in his mind he was looking forward to developing that roll of film with the unauthorized photo of me inside young King Tutankhamun's Tomb.

Tomorrow we would be boarding the train again for Aswan, five hours south of Luxor and I would be saying farewell to Hatshepsut.

The morning desert air was cool and the sun was barely peeking its red head over the horizon as we boarded the train for the next leg of our trip down the Nile to the lush city of Aswan.

As I sat on the train looking out the window I

realized that life from a distance is not always what it appears to be. The lush ribbon of green along the Nile in some areas was only just that, a narrow fertile strip of land that existed only as far as the eye could see. Beyond that would be hot white sand or red rocky terrain. Only this narrow band of land nourished by the water would feed the people and animals that lived in mud houses nearby.

Just like my life years ago, I thought. From a distance my career and marriage were what others wished to have. But the reality was just beyond the green; a tortured family behind a façade others envied.

We arrived at Aswan, a lush oasis in the middle of the desert around noon. Aswan is situated on the East Bank of the Nile and it is this place for centuries where cargoes had to be carefully navigated around the granite rocks beneath the surface of the deep waters. During our trip through Egypt we had many diverse desert landscapes, but Aswan seemed a paradise lost within the walls of sand, isolating it from the reality of a dry and monotone universe. Sands cover each side of the Nile in Aswan. That, coupled with the hot, dry air nurtured the tranquil atmosphere of a resort town.

As we stepped from the train the air was scented with the frail fragrance of mixed greenery. An unexpected pleasantry in the middle of such an arid land. My senses were pleased, indeed.

Arthur, Lee and I choose to walk the short distance from the train to the Old Cataract Hotel, a grand old dame sitting royally on the edge of a rocky granite cliff jetting up from the Nile.

A sea of feluccas, the broad, flat boats with their high gaff and single sail dotted the water below letting the warm breeze glide them along. Certainly a picturesque setting. There was something so peaceful about this place.

We had been told by our guide that the hotel had been used as a backdrop for the film of Agatha Christie's "Death on the Nile." I could understand why. The sight of her truly stirred the visual spirits within my imagination. The neatly painted white trim on the many windows contrasted well with her deep brick face. And the tall palms with their dark green spreading fronds reaching up toward the clear al lazward blue sky framed a picture even the best of filmmakers would covet.

Within the hotel our rooms didn't disappoint us either and the view was just as picturesque. From our window and across the Nile in front of us on the West Bank atop a hill we could see the famous tomb of Aga Kahn III, who had been the spiritual leader of the Ismailis during my lifetime. I first heard about him when his playboy son, Ali Kahn married our own Hollywood princess, Rita Hayworth. If my memory is correct, I do think Aga out-lived his high-profile son Ali, even though by all standards of good health versus longevity, the great Aga was not a good role model. He was more than a tad overweight.

Lunch was served in the large high-ceiling dining room with Nubians tending to the service of the meal. I watched their tall dark bodies move gracefully about the room, sweeping from table to table with their long legs camouflaged under their native galabyyas. The full length garments were fashioned in the baladi, or peasant style with wide sleeves and low rounded openings which exposed their long, proud mahogany necks. I thought of our stay in Luxor and our Nubian escort at the hotel there.

Since Aswan is the heart of the Nubian kingdom, he had surely uprooted from here and traveled north for some reason.

It was hard for me to understand why someone would leave his family and such a tranquil tropical place and venture beyond into the great wave of desert, or even north along the Nile where it was to always so peaceful. Could he have had an adventurer's soul? Been driven by his own dreams, as I had been as a child?

I mentally chastised myself for being so short-sighted lest I forget the lure of my own dreams. Forgive me, my Nubian friend. I do understand.

After lunch we were to take the circuit tour south of Aswan to the unfinished obelisk measuring over 27 ml. and rooted deeply into the bedrock.

The unfinished work, had it been completed would have been the largest piece of stone carved in history. A flaw was discovered in the stone so the project was abandoned. Like my husbands, I thought, mentally patting myself on the shoulder for ironically trying to get back my sense of humor. I know Arthur would have a field day with his camera, having us lean, stand on, or by, or measured up to the massive unfinished work of pink granite. Arthur had us doing everything but standing on our heads for the best photo opportunity.

From there we were to go to the Aswan Dam which was completed in 1971 and has enough metal in it to build 17 Eiffel Towers, or so Oham told us. Not that I could in my wildest imagination project that bizarre image to my brain, other than to remember the tourist stands in Paris with miniature Eiffels lined up by the hundreds, side by side. No photographs were allowed at the Aswan Dam, so Lee and I were spared the torture of leaning over the edge to get that 'great shot of a lifetime' in Egypt.

The dam *was* spectacular, though. A huge artificial lake, Lake Nasser, encompassing 500 km and reaching all the way to the Second Cataract in the Sudan, is created by the dam. Were it ever to erupt, we are told there would be a massive tidal wave that would wash down the Nile valley with great destruction and devastation to anything and everything in its powerful path. Just the sound of the water exploding would be deafening. A rather sobering thought in these times of world tsunamis and terrorism.

All photo opportunities denied, one by one we again boarded our yellow bus, each of us by now having laid claim to a favorite seat. Lee hardly ever sat with us. He preferred the back of the bus that usually was ignored by us older folk not too fond of the harder ride just beyond the rear wheels.

As we pulled away from the Cataract, I looked back and thought that maybe he was the smartest one after all. He was stretched out with his backpack under his head, settling down for an afternoon snooze in the privacy of his own space, while the rest of us were squeezed two by two in neat rows with little room to stretch our legs. I poked Arthur and motioned for him to turn and look at our son.

"Ah, never under estimate the wisdom of youth," he responded as he squirmed to get comfortable in his seat. Let's not forget that! That space is mine coming back!"

We visited several other tombs that afternoon, but their names or importance have since escaped me. I'm sure they were interesting and we did learn something, but somewhere between the Aswan Dam and the Old Aswan Dam built by the British in the late 1800's, my brain must have clicked off. The only thing I do remember is that Lee beat Arthur to the long, luxurious and private back seat on the bus.

"Youth must be served," I said as I slid into the seat next to the window to allow Arthur to stretch his long old legs out in the aisle of the narrow bus. "Let us not forget that!"

I returned, and saw under the sun, that the race is not
To the swift, nor the battle to the strong, neither yet
Bread to the wise, nor yet riches to men of Understanding, nor yet favor to men of skill, but Time and chance happened to them all.
—The Holy Bible Song of Solomon—

The Encounter

Our driver headed back along the dusty road toward Aswan. We had been on the road driving back to the hotel for just a short time and I was fascinated by the colors of the houses of the Nubian village we were traveling through.

Some of the square mud houses were painted bright yellow with equally bright blue doors.

65

Along the edges of the square houses in the front where the walls joined together, white trim had been painted in a vertical line from the roof to the ground. Some of the windows also had been framed with paint in this fashion. Other homes had very gay child-like murals drawn in primary red and blue and white next to the door and sometimes reaching to the white border at the edge of the front wall. Even the unpainted gray-brown mud houses had bright blue doors and the same white painted window trim.

Old tractors sat untouched and small piles of straw were all about in the bleached earthen yards. There were no fences, just piles of stones now and then about four feet high to make short extensions that were attached to the houses.

And donkeys. Donkeys everywhere. Usually where there was a donkey I could also see a child, either riding bare- backed or with a blanket saddle. Sometimes the donkey would be pulling a cart made of an old drum fitted with an axle and wheels. Poverty and need create such genius, I thought. I guess we all do manage in our way.

I wanted to be able to get a closer look at the children's faces, but they were too far away and just a part of the passing landscape.

My thoughts were interrupted by the jerk and sputter of our bus. We realized that something was definitely wrong when our driver coaxed it slowly along the road, with the engine hesitating in sputters. We heard the sound of steam escaping and then it died. The driver opened the bus door and climbed out to investigate under the hood. "Don't get off the bus," he ordered, "and keep the windows closed for now." He assured us that he would have it going in minutes. We weren't so sure.

Yours to God's ears, I thought. With the windows up and the heat outside, I knew it was going to get hot in the bus quickly.

Arthur moved to the front to get a closer look at the situation and I gazed out the window. I could see that by now the children knew we had stopped and we were becoming the day's curiosity.

Quickly it looked as though I was going to get my wish after all. The little faces were coming closer in full view of the bus. They each had firm little bodies tanned by the sun. One boy had a strap tee shirt and shorts on. Another wore a dusty galabiyya. All were in bare feet. Some came running toward us by foot. Some came by donkey. All came in cautious wonder.

But the one I remember most was a young girl, I suppose about eight years old. Her skin was the color of milk chocolate and her face was round and sweet. She was dressed in a faded cotton long dress that was stretched above her muddy knees as she straddled her white donkey. Her garment was open at the neck and exposed the edge of a white undershirt underneath. Her dark coarse hair was flying at all angles in the air and she squinted up at me from her vantage point outside the bus.

I looked down at her on her donkey that was loaded on each side with large earthen water pots. She was holding a big round can with Arabic script on it in yellow, white and blue. Favorite Nubian colors, I noted. The top of the can was removed and she it clutched securely at the rim. I wondered about its use as we gazed at each other. I from the security of the hot yellow bus and she from the security of that she knew. This was her home and whoever these strange faces were, we did not belong there.

I couldn't help but smile to her from my window. She was sizing me up I could tell, but she only continued to look at me with her serious dark brows knit together.

The driver boarded the bus and turned the starter. It connected and the roar of the engine garnered applause from its anxious riders.

I looked out to see if my little friend was still there. At least she isn't afraid to have gotten this close to us, I thought. I saw that she and her donkey had moved nearer. One more try as the bus started to move. I smiled again. Her little brown face broke into a slow grin and I could see that she had accepted my trust and shared a wonder about the other with me. I gave a slight wave as we drove off and left her and the other children standing by the dusty road.

That evening as my son and I were sitting on the terrace at the Old Cataract Hotel watching the sun set, showing only its golden crown as it slowly slipped behind the hill across the Nile. I thought of that brave little child and hoped that Allah would allow her a good life.

After loving you so much, can I
Forget you for eternity, and have no other
choice?
—*Robert Traill Spence Lowell*—

The Story of Elizabeth

Music? I must have been dreaming. I opened my eyes and for a second wasn't quite sure where we were. My eyes focused on the light of a new day filtering through the slats in the louvers covering our windows.

Singing?

I heard it again and it seemed to be coming from outside the window. I looked over at

Arthur's sleeping form and quietly slipped out from beneath the covers and with my feet searched around to connect with my slippers. Mission accomplished, I shuffled across the room and opened the shutters to investigate further the source of the sounds.

The pale face of the morning sun was barely visible, the morning rays casting short shadows on the Nile below our hotel room as the parade of feluccas on its waters was beginning for the day. The boatmen manning the tall sails were singing their songs to the River of Life and Allah.

A soft breeze was blowing and I took a deep breath and filled my lungs with the warm aromatic air, the rush of its oxygen heightening my senses.

This country is so beautiful, I thought as I watched the feluccas flit around below like butterflies trying to find the slightest whisper of wind to carry them along on their flight down river.

I felt myself changing during this trip. The experience in Luxor had changed something within me. I am like a butterfly, too, I mused. A woman with many lives like the legs of a caterpillar, and in my prime imprisoned in a cocoon. Am I now free to escape from my own self-spun analogous structure that I sealed tightly to protect me from harm? Emerge from my prison with the wings of freedom to carry me to places beyond my wildest dreams? Dart about the Nile, rest among the tall palms and perhaps sit on Ramses nose for awhile. The thought of this preposterous fantasy made me giggle aloud and I turned to see if I had awakened Arthur.

Too much oxygen I thought as I slid back into bed and cuddled up next to my husband. I closed my eyes and took comfort in the peacefully sleeping form next to me and listened to the boatmen's morning serenades below. Today we would be free to do what we wanted in Aswan and we could sleep in for once.

By ten we were all up, had eaten breakfast and were headed for a walk along the Corniche where we would be able to look across the Nile and see the dark cave-like holes that were in reality ancient tombs of Aswan's nobles.

Elephantine Island and the Ferial Gardens and a visit to the nearby Coptic Church were as much as we could handle by afternoon, so we headed back to the Old Cataract for lunch and an afternoon nap. I set the alarm to awaken us early enough so we could take our places on the balcony for another view of the sunset over the Nile and the feluccas and their boatmen playing in the sunset.

The cool of the evening would be reserved for a trip to the Sharia El Souk, the main bazaar street of Aswan and they say the best bazaar outside of Cairo. We had not seen too much of Cairo yet, that would be covered on the last leg of our journey, so we couldn't compare. But we truly had a great time wandering through the bazaar and sampling its wares.

Arthur and I had galabiyyas made for us with our cartouches on them. We would have time in the morning to pick them up before we boarded the train to go back up the Nile to Cairo.

Lee bought an Arabian head covering and we all sampled some freshly baked flat bread so warm and flavorful and that tasted like none other I have had since.

The market was lively and crowded that night

and we walked along the bazaar in wonder of all the energy of trade flowing along the streets.

The next morning we all awoke early to the felucca chorus, had breakfast and headed back to the bazaar to pick up our galabiyyas that were promised to be made to order for us overnight.

We turned right from the main street and walked along the bazaar. How different everything looked in the light of day. The night before the narrow streets were filled with people, either buying or selling their wares. The mood was one that reminded me of what in ancient times a typical market place must have been; full of life and the excitement that the matching of wits between buyer and seller brings, each wanting to leave with the best price and the sense of victory that comes with it.

It was early and many of the shops were yet to open and we hoped that we had not misunderstood our merchant that our purchases would be ready by morning. In the daylight we had little difficulty finding the narrow winding street that lead us to the small stall shop that only had room enough for two old sewing machines and its occupants; two elderly men dressed in native pheasant clothing, their dark skin weathered by age and the dry desert sun.

They both smiled and waved us into their shop and displayed for our approval the galabiyyas we had ordered. They motioned for me to feel the cloth from which they were made. I took the edge of one garment and felt the softness of the fine Egyptian cotton. I smiled and indicated my approval. The rituals of a satisfactory exchange being completed, we quickly walked back to the hotel to make ready for our journey back up the Nile to Cairo.

What a wonderful stay it has been here, I thought, as the train slowly moved from the station toward our destination. Having spent time absorbing the culture of this country, perhaps clarity and meaning for me heightened, traveling up the river as it flows along in the opposite direction.

It is tragic to be poor in any country, yet here the schisms between classes have been deeply etched for thousands of years. I could see little chance of anyone escaping the lot of the draw-

unto whom you were born. That is where you will be in this life. My dreams for the brave little Nubian girl I viewed from the bus would in all reality be just that. Only dreams.

Once again I watched the landscape from my window focusing on each image trying to imprint them in my mind forever. I didn't want to forget the things I had learned here, the emotions that I had felt. The centuries of living along these waters add a spiritual richness to this land and its people. I gazed intently at each passing scene, then slowly fell into a deep sleep as the train moved along. Something I had never before been able to do in my entire life.

I don't know how long I had been sleeping, but when I awoke, Arthur and Lee were not in our compartment. I looked at my watch, Four o'clock! It couldn't be. How could I have slept so long! I spotted a note on the seat opposite me. *'We're in the club car. 3:00 Arthur'*

I got up and freshened my face and tied back my unruly hair. I still felt a little groggy. The thought of a strong cup of French coffee really appealed to me, so I forced myself to make my way to where the boys were in the club car. I needed to inject my body with a little caffeine to get me fully charged again.

The club car was filled with passengers. I could hear the mix of many languages in friendly conversations, laughter and the sounds of people having a good time. Through the thick smoke I could see in the far corner a group of people singing and a man playing a concertina. It reminded me of a carload of slightly tipsy people coming home from a great party.

I found the boys sitting by the window playing cards with two other passengers. I thought it best not to disturb them in the middle of what might be a great hand, so I made my way to the bar and ordered a cup of coffee. I looked around for a place to sit and found an empty chair in a small area on the right side of the car next to an older woman apparently engrossed in an interesting book. I hated to disturb her, but I had no choice.

"Do you mind?" I asked gesturing to the empty chair next to her.

"What?...Oh. No...I mean...Yes, that's quite all right," she said softly in a refined English accent. She took off her reading glasses and smoothed her tinted red hair that had been disturbed by the uprooting of her glasses. She must have been deeply involved in her reading. I quickly studied her round colorful face as I seated myself.

"I didn't mean to disturb you, but my husband and son are playing cards over there and all I'm interested in right now is a serious cup of coffee."

She put down her book, folded her reading glasses and inserted them between its pages as a marker.

"Really, that's quite all right. I was just reading to pass the time. I'm traveling by myself and books are suitable companions I find, even when dining alone. One doesn't have to pick up their cheque and the conversations are most delightful."

I smiled and nodded in agreement. How clever she is. Immediately I wanted to know more about her, but I didn't want to invade her privacy.

"I'm on a holiday of sorts," she volunteered. "My grandfather came to Aswan from England as a young man to help build the Old Aswan Dam in 1889. He fell in love with the country, went home and his stories inspired my father so, that when he received his degree from the university he came here to work. My father worked for the British as an engineer for years."

"Wasn't it hard on your mother, being so far away from home for such a long time?" I asked thinking of my own life.

"Mother never lived here. My father fell in love with a beautiful young Egyptian girl from a very wealthy family. Father was very dashing and well-educated, but it didn't matter. He as a foreigner and an Englishman to boot. They were very much in love, but her family would have none of it and they sent her away. He tried to find her, but had no luck…"

"How awful! He must have been devastated."

"He was. I suspect her family was also very powerful politically, for soon after Father was called home to England by the government. He left vowing to come back to find her, but his papers were never renewed. He never could return."

"Then he must have met your mother later." I waited for her to continue.

"He knew her before, but she was very young when he left for Egypt."

"Oh. Then how did he meet her again?"

"My mother was the vicar's daughter. Naturally, Father was beside himself when he returned home and lost all will to go about living again. So much so that he even lost his beliefs."

"In God, or life?"

"No doubt, both," she emphasized.

" My grandfather, the vicar, took pity upon my poor father and gave him the spiritual encouragement to carry on. And in time, as my mother blossomed into womanhood, my father slowly fell in love with her. My mother may have healed his broken heart, but he never forgot his Egyptian love."

"What makes you say that?" I wondered if her mother had sensed his distance at times as I have done with Arthur.

"Well, I didn't even know about her until after my father died. Mother never mentioned her to me, either. Father outlived Mother and was lost without her. No one could console him, not even me. He died soon after. No apparent cause. I'm convinced now he died of a broken heart. After loosing both of the loves of his life he didn't care to go on."

81

"Is that possible?" I was a little skeptical.

"Yes, of course. Medical science has indicated so in many cases."

I sipped my coffee as she continued.

"After he died and as part of his will, he left a sealed envelope with instructions that it was to go to me and opened only after my mother's death, should he pass before her. I was indeed curious, but I could not gather the fortitude to open it immediately. I was still mourning for my mother and now my father. It was too much, just too much for me at the time. I wasn't ready."

I understood. How many times I had postponed reality because I couldn't face it at that moment. "But, of course, you eventually did?"

"Yes. I did in time." She motioned for the waiter to come.

"I'm having a cup of tea. Would you care for more coffee?"

"No. I'm fine, thank you." Was that a signal that she doesn't want to finish her story?

"Would you like to continue your reading, I didn't mean for you to stop…"

"Aren't you a little curious about the letter?"

She smiled mischievously at me as the waiter brought her tea and placed it on the small round table near her closed book.

"Well, yes, of course, very curious." I replied honestly. The caffeine had finally kicked in and I was wide awake.

"After some time, I did open the letter. As I pulled the letter from its envelope a small gold necklace fell from it. I recognized right away it was a cartouche, but didn't know the name. In the letter itself my father related his story about the Egyptian girl and told me that the necklace belonged to her. Her name was Bastet. His instructions to me were to travel to Egypt and return the necklace to her. He asked me to find Bastet, but should it be that she was not alive, or I could not find her, then his instructions to me were, and I use his exact words, '...Take her necklace to Aswan and at sunset from a felucca in the middle of the Nile give it its freedom. Tell the River of Life to find her and return it to Bastet.' She paused and took a sip of tea.

"Did you do it? Did you go...or find her?"

"Yes and no," she replied.

"What do you mean?"

"Well, I found her family. Her father had

arranged a marriage for her one year after my father returned to England. This marriage produced one child, a daughter, named Fathama. By the time I had made my journey, Bastet had died. I found Fathama at the University in Cairo. She was a lovely woman. A professor of philosophy, quite emancipated, although it didn't surprise me."

"Yes, your mother certainly took some independent steps to even dare to fall in love with your father, especially in those days."

"Well, I took a chance and told her my story and in the end I went against my father's wishes. I didn't give the Nile Bastet's cartouche. I gave it to Fatima, her daughter."

"You were right. I would have done the same thing. Did you ever see her again?"

"Oh, yes. We're both alone now, you see, but through our parents, we now have each other. She comes to England for a holiday whenever she can and I visit her here once a year. It's really been splendid, you know. Like having a long lost sister."

"What a touching story. But I have to ask one more thing, if I may. What were you doing in Aswan? Didn't you say Fathama lives in Cairo?"

"Yes. But over the years I continued to feel guilty about not honoring my father's wish about the cartouche. Then Fathama and I came up with a solution that is most marvelous that I think Father would have approved of. Brilliant really. Yesterday in Aswan, just before sunset I took a felucca out into the Nile and as the sun was setting behind Elephantine Island, I dropped my father's university ring into the water and asked the Nile to carry it to Bastet..."

Suddenly Arthur and his booming voice were commanding center stage, hovering above me. "When did you get here? We thought you were still asleep and we're on our way to get you."

"Hey, Mother! We thought you were going to sleep all day!"

"For your information, I've been here for a long time, but you were playing cards and I didn't want to disturb you."

"Sure, Mother, we know," Lee said trying to get a rise out of me.

My companion jumped in, "She has, truly. I can vouch for her. I am afraid I am the one who had been taking up all of her time. You both can blame me."

All of a sudden I realized that I now knew so

much about her, but I did not know my storyteller's name. "I'm sorry, I didn't introduce you…"

"That's quite all right. I'm Elizabeth."

"And this is my husband, Arthur, and my son, Lee….I'm Sandra."

Elizabeth looked at Lee and Arthur and then to me. "I know you realize how lucky you are to have such a handsome husband and fine son. We mustn't take things of that sort for granted now, must we," she said giving my arm a gentle pat.

"Won't you join us for dinner, Elizabeth? We'd love to have you," invited Arthur.

I fortified the invitation. "Yes. Please Elizabeth. It would be our pleasure."

"Thank you, you are most kind, but I have had a rather tiring trip this time. The best medicine for this old girl now is a hot toddy and an early turn in." With that she picked up her book and rose from her chair.

I truly was disappointed. I wanted to spend more time with her. I reached for her free hand and grasped it. "Thank you, Elizabeth." I knew she somehow understood.

She smiled and winked at me and walked out

of the club car.

I'm not really sure whether Elizabeth's story was true or taken from the pages of one of her faithful companions. It doesn't matter. Her tale had made me realize how important it is to appreciate the gift of love while we have it.

I slid my hand into Arthur's and took hold of my son's.

"I love you both so much...don't you ever forget it. Now, shall we dine?" I asked in my best English accent.

Nothing ever becomes real till it
Is experienced—
Even a proverb is no Proverb to you till your
Life has illustrated it.
—John Keats—

Saying Good-bye

By sunset we arrived at our hotel in Cairo, a thin sliver of a building squeezed into a crowded urban landscape with narrow and winding streets. Two armed soldiers in black uniforms, their sleeves buttoned at the wrists in spite of the oppressive heat, flanked the doorway.

"Man, look at those guys!" Lee was already sizing up their weapons.

"All the comforts of home," Arthur murmured looking their way, "You suppose they're to watch us or protect us..."

I was beginning to feel a little unsettled.
"Probably a little of both. We're all Western tourists, but we did come on an Israeli tour, you know."

The driver unloaded our baggage from the bus and we went ahead with the group into the hotel. The lobby looked very European with overstuffed chairs and dark leather couches with tall table lamps standing in sentry beside them.

The narrow room was filled with a mixture of faces, tourists from America and Western Europe, as well as the Middle East.

Arthur and Lee volunteered to go to the desk to check in and I found a place in one of the well-worn chairs. My feet were still sore from our arduous walk along the Aswan Cornice and the bazaar the day before. I was determined to get first dibs on the tub that night, if there was one.

My eyes moved about the room. I noticed a man dressed in white Arabian garments with a black cord securing his head dress standing near the couch in the center of the lobby. Behind him stood four Arabic women of various ages. They all were dressed very finely and I imagined them to be his family, either wives or a combination of wives and daughters. Their faces were veiled and only their dark eyes were visible to those who dared look at them.

I wanted to catch a full glimpse of their eyes, hoping to connect somehow just for a moment, but their glances were only for each other. Sisterhood. In their male-dominated society, I understood that they only had one another to trust and that they had been drawn together by Allah in service to their husband or father. I wondered if they secretly longed for freedom, or were they content with the only way of life that they were allowed.

Knowledge is not always the answer for everyone, I thought. In some cases, as tragic as it may seem, sometimes there may be less pain in acceptance.

Our hotel in Cairo was not exactly five star, but it was equipped with the most modern conveniences we had experienced yet, even television. The rooms and windows were small and lacked the charm of the other hotels we had stayed in during our trip down the Nile, but it had a modern shower and tub that I knew I could soak in for hours.

We were so tired from the days spent sight-seeing and climbing over every tomb and ruin that time would allow. My usually fair skin was now a golden brown, except for my face that I protected from the strong rays of the desert sun with a straw hat. It was very unusual for me to be sporting a tan, but early during our trip I had given up hiding from the sun. It was just impossible.

We had dinner with our tour guide and excused ourselves early and eagerly went up to our room for a night of television and, for me, a luxurious evening in a warm bath. I closed the door behind me, shook a few drops of my precious Channel No.5 into the hot bath and let the room fill with perfumed steam, shutting out the world.

So far my journey to this mystic and beautiful land had brought with it many new discoveries. I was delighting in the wonders of a civilization long past and marveling at new life in the urban areas. But the greatest discovery is that here I had visited many new places within myself that

I had locked away for years. The excavation of old memories was having a cleansing effect on me. I knew I was experiencing a catharsis that was well overdue. It was too soon to tell where it would take me, but I was willing to let go and let it happen. I knew that night I would sleep well.

Cock-a-doodle-doo. Cock-a-doodle-doo.

This is crazy. I looked over at the clock. Five!

Cock-doodle-do. Cock-a-doodle-doo.

The early morning light was just beginning to break through the night as I peered out the open window to investigate the crows that to my ears sounded like roosters. How many times I had heard that familiar sound when living on my grandpa's farm. But in the middle of Cairo? I don't think so.

Cock-a-doodle-doo!

The sounds echoed again through the morning light. I focused my eyes toward the direction of the crowing. No. Nothing. Then as the light of morning slowly lifted, I spotted a roof-full of chickens and roosters to the left of our hotel. Urban farming! What next!

"Sandra?" Arthur whispered half-asleep.

"Over here. By the window," I answered.

"Wa'da you doing there?" he drawled groggily. "Can't sleep?"

"I'm beginning to have a passion for hotel windows."

"Okay." He rolled over and fluffed his pillow. "Don't jump without kissing me goodbye. Promise?"

"Very funny. Don't you hear the roosters? Listen."

"Are you crazy? We are in a twelve story hotel in the middle of Cairo. Come back to bed."

"No. Honestly. I'm not kidding. The roof below has a chicken farm on it. Great picture opportunity."

I had said the magic words. Arthur slid out of bed and shuffled to the window.

"Look. Over there to the left." I pointed to the

roof below.

"Well, I'll be..", he murmured as he happily reached for his camera.

"And do you see that pyramid over there? It looks like it is pretty close, doesn't it...at least very near."

He was right. The breaking dawn exposed the outline of a great pyramid that was off to the left of us on the far horizon. The sight was both amazing and contradictory. Modern buildings, rooftop farms, and pyramids all within the eye of the camera lens. Click. In one mille-second Arthur had captured what had taken thousands of years to evolve.

I watched him in his stripped pajamas and morning hair going every which way, leaning out the window with his camera. I know you I thought, but do I *really* know you? You know me, you think you do, but *do* you?

I wanted to pull him in and put my arms around him and tell him how much I loved him. To tell him how hard it was for me to trust love again and to please wait. In time.

Free to feel. Free to Trust. Free to believe that every morning when I wake up he will be there. I was still a prisoner of my past. Locked away from my feelings. I quietly watched him click away then slipped between the smooth Egyptian cotton sheets looking forward to the start of a new day.

After an early breakfast we headed for the bus again to drive the long road from our hotel in downtown Cairo to the suburb of Giza. Then to the great plateau to visit the pyramid of Cheops, the largest of the three remaining Giza pyramids and the ones we saw from our hotel window.

Again in my childhood journeys through the National Geographic, I was introduced to pyramids through pictures of these very same Wonders of the World at Giza. They were grand, even more so than I had imagined.

It is estimated that this group of pyramids were built between 2600 BC and 2525 BC and that they were constructed so that they would be in direct alignment with the North Star. That is only one of many opinions, of course. The mystery of the great pyramids at Giza have given speculation from many authorities over the years and conflicting opinions as to how and why they were so constructed.

The skies held great importance in the ancient times, both mystical and practical for the Egyptians. The stars were important for sea and land travel and also held the power of the Gods. But other Egyptologists believe that mathematical importance influenced the construction of the pyramids. Will we ever really know the truth?

Around 3100 BC both the upper and lower regions of Egypt were united under the rule of Menes who established the first dynasty. He made Memphis the seat of his rule. Menes was the creator of the step pyramid, a succession of tombs, one on top of the other, the smaller ones on top, creating a triangular shape structure. All of the pyramids that housed the tombs of the dead pharaohs were made to last for more than their earthly lifetime, therefore, they were built of blocks of limestone and encased with polished stone on each of the exterior three sides.

Very unlike the mud houses we had seen all along the Nile and through the desert that were meant to last an earthly lifetime. Oham explained to us that the ancient homes built for the living were built only for the time span of life as it was here on earth, therefore, they were made of mud bricks. Death was more eternal, so the pyramids were made of limestone blocks to ensure the longevity of the protection of the tombs. The pyramids were to house not only the eternal, but the spiritual lives of the pharaohs.

As I looked up in awe at the enormous size of the pyramid of Cheops, I wondered if the secrets of this grand monument would ever be authenticated or even agreed upon.

The area around the base of the pyramids was quite crowded with a mixture of tourists with their cameras and camels with their drivers. The eclectic sights were quite entertaining to Lee and I, and as usual, provided Arthur with great subject matter for his lens.

"Want to ride on a camel around the pyramids?" Arthur shouted from his photo opportunity spot near the base of the Cheops pyramid.

"Who? Me? You've got to be kidding!" I said pulling my hat further down on my head to keep out the sun. "That is one experience I will never regret missing!"

'Oh, come on. Be a sport. The driver holds the reins, you won't get hurt."

I pinched my nose with my fingers. "Have you ever smelled those things!"

With that he and Lee hopped on the big ugly beast. Arthur wanted a picture of him and my son on the camel because when he was there with the Merchant Marines at Port Said a hundred years ago when he was eighteen he had one taken. After I clicked to capture the historical moment, I handed the camera back to Arthur and away they went into the sunset with the camel driver holding the reins.

No way, I thought, as I watched them bounce away on their long-legged transport. I was going into the pyramid. I wanted to see the King's Chambers. I would meet them near the Sphinx.

Little did I know then, but I snapped the now famous picture of Arthur and Lee astride a camel in front of the famous Cheops that sits on his dresser next to the Port Said shot.

I quickly walked toward the pyramid to begin my voyage into the belly of the ancient beast. This one skillfully and firmly rooted in the desert for thousands of years.

As I entered through the narrow doorway into the pyramid, I felt like Alice slipping though the keyhole into Wonderland. The bright sunlight disappeared as we stepped through the narrow opening and into eternal darkness. Dim lights strung along the way above our heads guided our steps up the long ascending corridor that was to lead us to the King's Chamber. The air was stale and I found myself taking shallow breaths to avoid filling my lungs with the unpleasant substance.

As we climbed further into the dark mass, the passageway became frighteningly low and narrow and I struggled as I fought off claustrophobia. My heart began to pump harder as the space before, behind, below and above me became more constricted. My feet searched to find safe footing on the chicken ramps beneath me. The narrow slats horizontally nailed to the long boards were worn with use and made it difficult to be sure of my footing. The ascent became steeper and I worked hard to focus against panic. Surely we were almost there. The lower I had to bend and the steeper I had to climb, made the choice of a camel ride instead of this, better and better.

Finally, a small opening ahead appeared and one by one we slipped through the doorway and one by one stretched our bodies back into a standing position.

I looked around the room. It was a plain square space except for an open sarcophagus that was also empty. Nothing. Just an empty room with nothing written on the walls. No story to tell us about this king, Cheops. Nothing.

It has been told that when Napoleon visited the King's Chamber, upon his exit from his journey into the pyramid he said he did not want to speak of it anymore.

It is my theory that he either was humbled by an attack of claustrophobia, or else he had the same reaction as I. Is that all there is?

Of course, had the tomb raiders not gotten there before us, it would have been another story.

The downward trip seemed much less painful and frightening. I knew by then what to expect. I followed the others in a single file, crouching down and carefully securing my footing as before. Soon we were at the opening and out into the sun and fresh, fresh air again. As I stepped out from the cool, dank edifice and down from the large block of limestone onto the sand, the August heat torched my body as though I had just walked into a volcano.

I found Lee and Arthur at the Sphinx, both of them still smelling a bit like camel. I tried to stay upwind, but it was rather hopeless. There was only a slight movement of air in the desert afternoon heat, so there was little I could do other than walk in front of them.

The Sphinx was much smaller than we had expected. Somehow I had envisioned this great Cleopatra-like edifice sans beard to be much larger than it actually is. The beard, we're told, was now in the British Museum. Its nose was also missing, thanks to the fourteenth century Turks who supposedly used it for target practice and in the process had obliterated its nose.

Boys will be boys. Nothing ever changes does it? I thought as I looked at the scarred and eroded face of this famous monument. It could be restored. That kind of damage can be fixed. No psychological elements to deal with. Emotional healing, on the other hand, is a slow process. No quick fix for that. Slap on some glue and paint and you'll be just fine. If only it were that easy.

I began thinking of my children, I guess all children, and how like the Sphinx anchored in a bed of limestone, the bulk of their growth is rooted deeply into the lives of their parents as it unfolds and they are captive to the events surrounding them. They have no choice. That's the saddest part. Each generation brings their own load to the lives of their children. It is never ending and the cycle is repeated in some version over and over again.

It always has been amazing to me that the longer I live, the more I realize that although time passes, much stays the same. There really is nothing new under the sun, just new twists.

Fashions come and go. If you save something long enough, it is sure to return to be in style again. Maybe in a different color spectrum, or with a slightly different sleeve, but guaranteed it will return with a twist.

War is here to stay. It doesn't matter where you live in the world, in your country, in your town, or with your next door neighbor. There will always be conflict as long as we like the power of owning things, want boundaries, and we are passionate about personal beliefs.

Oh, there will be peace, too. Without war you cannot have peace. So that is a guarantee that peace is here to stay, now and then. First here and then over there. And then the cycle will repeat itself. Guaranteed.

There will always be a new Wonder of the World, only different in size or location and if it is built, people will come to see and to wonder at its greatness. And as long as there is life on this planet there will be a God of some sort and an afterlife of some kind and an eternal reward we can look forward to. If we live long enough, we will see that cycle repeat itself. Life and death of all things. Over and over again.

Like the mud walls in the basement of my parent's old house that was a part of John Brown's underground railway during the American Civil War. It has seen life and death repeat itself many times. This Sphinx, too, would have much to say of what it has seen if it could. And perhaps some four-letter words for those Turks who messed with his nose.

Arthur's camera can freeze moments of time and capture memories for us, but those moments that slip through our fingers like the tiny prisms of desert sand, are lost forever as they drop away unnoticed into a body of sameness. If I had known it was going to be so special and to move so fast, I would have held on to it longer. Ah. If only we had the power.

I was still deep in my own thought as we sat in the Sound and Light Pavilion watching the sun set and waiting for the light show. The sphinx was the narrator of this much heralded event. I guess the Sphinx has a voice after all, I thought.

It was starting to get cold and I was glad that we had all brought sweaters to protect us from the evening desert chill. We had only one more night left in Egypt and I wanted to be sure that these moments would be special. I wanted to hold on to them.

The night sky in the Middle East is so clear and dark. The sky is lit with trillions of stars and there is very little ground light to interfere with the reflections of the celestial illumination. It was quite spectacular to see this heavenly display on such a clear Egyptian evening. This night we were sitting and admiring the surrounding beauty of the sky, brilliant stars and the great wonders of the world. As I sat there, the light show told the story of ancient Egypt and the pyramids and it was as though ancient and modern times had joined together with the ancient Sphinx in this modern artistic display of lights and narration.

As I sat there listening to the story coming from the base of the Great Sphinx, I thought of my chance meeting on the train with Elizabeth and being witness to the tale she told about true love. I really wanted to believe that her story was true and I thought just maybe on our list of sights to see tomorrow, that I would drop by the University of Cairo and try to see if Fathama was a real person, or just a character from Elizabeth's beloved pages.

I knew that we would be leaving Cairo in two days, and a great sadness fell upon me. I wanted to go home, but also a part of me wanted to stay. I had found so much about myself here and had been able to release and begin to deal with memories that had long been buried deep within me.

The spiritual beauty of this land had allowed me to open memories that had been locked away for so many years. I had found places in my heart that I had forgotten existed. For this I will always be grateful.

Well this is the end of a perfect day,
Near the end of a journey, too.
—Carrie Jacobs Bond—

Fathama

Those last few days in Cairo, I kept thinking about the women whose paths I had crossed. Elizabeth's story was never far from my mind. And I could not forget the image of the beautiful Neubian child and the women in the sheik's harem. Hatshepsut. I felt I had much in common with these women. In spite of the evolution of time and our cultural differences-our joys, our pain, our suffering is universal. Womanhood crosses all barriers. We share the common denominator of being the nurturers of the universe, but even in our enlightened Western culture, it is still a man's world.

I hadn't shared Elizabeth's story with Arthur. I didn't think it would mean anything to him and I rather felt that it was something I wanted to keep for myself. Somehow I just didn't want to dilute the special story and I felt that quite possibly he would not be able to appreciate the entire concept of her story.

The last day in Cairo was spent touring numerous sights. I guess Oham wanted to pack in everything he could for us during our short stay there. We toured most of the Coptic, the El Moulalaqua Church, called the hanging church next to the Coptic Museum in Old Cairo. And the Abou-Serga Church not far from Moualaqua, said to mark the place where the Holy Family rested on the flight to Egypt.

The remainder of our day was spent touring the Islamic Cairo.

The Citadel of Salah-El-Din which is located in Eastern Cairo at the foot of the Mukattam Hill. This is a thirteenth century fortress. One of the buildings is the Mohammed Ali Mosque. Included in our day we also visited the Al Azhir Mosque and the university located in El-Hussein

Square which was founded in the tenth century. Al Azhir is the world's oldest university.

We visited the Coptic Museum in Old Cairo and then went back into Cairo, behind the Nile Hilton Hotel to visit the Egyptian Museum where King Tutankhamun treasures were on view.

We finished our tour of the university around lunchtime and we decided to independently seek lunch on our own and break away from the group.

"Arthur?" I asked as we walked along looking for a place to eat. I was gently approaching Arthur about trying to find Fathama.

"What?" He answered taking my hand as we continued walking.

"After lunch, I want to know if you would mind going over to the administration office at the university? I would like to inquire about something."

He gave me a puzzled look. "What are you looking for?"

"Well, you remember that woman on the train, Elizabeth?"

"Sure, What about her?"

"She told me that she had a very good friend

who was a teacher a the university…"

"So?" Arthur interrupted.

"So, I just thought I might like to see if she's really there."

"What do you care, you don't even know her and I'm sure she would be quite mystified if you caught up with her. What's this all about?"

"It's rather complicated, but Elizabeth told me this fascinating story and I got so involved in her narration about her life and the way it connected with this woman that I… Well, I just want to know if Elizabeth was just entertaining me or not. I want to know if this Fathama really exists."

"This all transpired while we were playing cards?
Is it that important to you? Why would you even care?"

"I don't know. Maybe I want to believe in fairy tales. Just somehow the story touched me and I wanted to find out, that's all."

"Oh-oh. It's the old newswoman nose again I think."

"Yeah, maybe, but, honestly, I'm just curious, that's all."

I admit I felt I was just a wee bit crazy, but

Arthur agreed since we had some free time after lunch that we would all walk over and let me do my detective work.

On the way we managed to find a small outdoor café and lunched on houmas and flat bread and drank very warm and very, very sweet Cokes.

At the University the guard pointed the way to the administration office and we climbed the steep steps to the second floor and entered the first door on the left.

The office was quite crowded due to the time of day. Most seemed to be students, some in modern western dress and some and some in traditional Egyptian clothing. I made my way to the front desk, by now feeling a little foolish and having second thoughts about my mission. It would be just awful if I ran into Elizabeth. Stranger things had happened to me in my lifetime. I was certain she would be able to see thought any lie I could quickly make up as to what brought me there.

Hoping that she could speak English, I waited at the desk until the young woman behind was free to speak to me and I asked if they had a teacher in the Philosophy Department by the first name of Fathama. I feigned that I couldn't remember her last name when in truth I didn't even know it.

"Would that be Dr. Fathama Alarahman? But she is not here and won't be back until tomorrow. Would you care to leave a message for her? I can put it in her box."

"Oh,. no thank you, that won't be necessary. We're leaving tomorrow." I replied.

I quickly thanked the pleasant young woman and walked away from the desk and through the door into the hallway where I had left Lee and Arthur.

"Well?" they both echoed as I came toward them, "Is she real?"

"Yep." I said with a smile. "She sure is. Thank you, Elizabeth!" I refused to take into account that Fathama is a common Egyptian name. In my heart, I wanted to believe.

I was ready to go home. My journey in Egypt was completed.

The Gift

Life evaporates in microscopic units
   unnoticed measures silently flowing.
A gentle surf stealing grains
   as it strokes the shores of each day.

Dichotomy.

Healer. Thief. Savior. Enemy.
Elusive. Manageable.

Ride the pendulum with wisdom
   your dreams and energy giving it movement.
Inertia measuring each returning swing
   in anticipation of its wonders.

Forget not one tick, not one swing.
Forget not your purpose, not your dreams.

Forget not mine.

Sandra Hart

Prologue

The good news is that the twice-mentioned Dr. Brown returned to our tour with a new passport and was able to continue with the group under the watchful eye of Oham until the end of the tour. And in retrospect, our 1984 tour was perhaps the beginning of the end of tourism in the Middle East as we knew it. At that time, we felt safe and free to wander about the country enjoying the life and sights as we experienced them. Unfortunately, this idyll was not to last

On November 17, 1997 at Luxor's Temple of Hatshepsut, where we had strolled casually, absorbing the wonders that I speak of in this journal, six Islamic militants armed with guns and knives and disguised as police, emerged from the nearby cliffs, firing randomly at tourists, killing sixty. Blood spattered the ancient colonnades, and sandstone pillars were marked by bullet holes and bits of flesh.

The Middle Court of the 3,500 year-old Temple of Hatshepsut, that had impressed me so much during my visit there, had become a late twentieth century slaughterhouse.

The UAE's Arabic-language press were united in their condemnation of the massacre.

A statement issued in the name of Egypt's most prominent Islamic militant group said the massacre had begun as an attempt to take hostages in order to secure the release of a leader imprisoned in New York for his role in the first World Trade Center bombing. But the accounts by survivors gave no hint of any efforts to take tourists alive.

In January of 2006, nine years after the Luxor incident and twenty-two years after our first visit to Egypt, Arthur and I boarded the stately Queen Elizabeth 2 in New York City for a 109 day Voyage of the Seven Wonders World Cruise.

The Queen Elizabeth 2 took us to twenty-seven countries and forty-two ports. Two of the ports on our itinerary were more or less a homecoming for us. We stopped at two Egyptian ports; Safaga and Alexandria. And in order to get from one to the other, we had to navigate through the Suez Canal.

I wasn't at all too sure that it might be best to let old memories remain sweet and lie as they are inside of me, rather than walk the terrain as I did back in 1984. This time with new insights and images to dilute my prior ones.

During the three months aboard the Queen Elizabeth 2 before we arrived at the Egyptian ports I had to think about what we were going to do. I finally decided that I wanted to remember Egypt as is was in my journals. I chose not to disturb the wonderful images I had of my travels over 20 years ago.

I wanted to remember the innocence and strong heritage I witnessed. I wanted to remember the warm reception given all over Egypt to us Americans. Right choice? For me, looking back at our decision, I think so. For on the return of the 2006 Queen Elizabeth tours, we learned that they traveled in caravan, bus behind bus, ten in all, lead by an emergency repair bus and each bus had security aboard.

In the port of Safaga we chose to visit a resort in this popular seaside holiday spot. The unspoiled beaches and strong breezes off the Red Sea made it the perfect site for us to unwind during the last leg of our cruise. We sat on white wooden chaises under big colorful umbrellas secured in the white sand. We read and swam and chatted with other voyagers that chose the beach instead of touring.

We lunched in an open dining area at the water's edge that clattered with German, Dutch, Arabic and English languages. We ate fresh fish from the Red Sea and devoured flat bread that was being baked by a native Safagan woman and placed in warm piles on the generous ledge of the brick oven.

Although Safaga's real lure is being the gateway to Egypt's powerful and mysterious past-the great Temple of Karnak, The Valley of the Kings and the ruins of Luxor Temple and Ramses I's great temple at Abu Simbel near Aswan. We had already experienced all of these and our day at this famed seaside resort was just the indulgence we needed. We went back to the ship fully rested and prepared for the final leg of our journey.

In Jordan we had planned a visit to the Rose City of Petra at the port of Aqaba, but because of security cautions, the Queen Elizabeth 2 headed directly toward the Suez Canal. Appreciative of the heightened security involving our travels in the Middle East, I couldn't help but be very disappointed at not being able to visit the lost city of Petra-a city that historians believe may date to 6,000 B.C. Also, nearby is Wadi Rum where T.E. Lawrence found his destiny as "Laurence of Arabia" and sparked the Arab Revolt of 1917.

In 1984 our tour bus drove onto a ferry and we passengers disembarked the bus to stand along the side of the ferry a portion of the long trip through the Suez Canal.

In 2006 the Queen Elizabeth 2 arrived early at the mouth of the canal to ensure a first spot going through. Much has changed since the casual navigation we had in1984. Our recent traversing of the Suez brought trucks of armed soldiers on both sides of the canal following to protect us the entire length of the canal. Armed boats also guided us through. I'm not sure if they were there the entire trip, or just at the beginning, but their armed presence symbolized today's era of terrorism in which we are enveloped. I can't speak highly enough of the security precautions taken by Cunard, the British, American and Egyptian governments to ensure our safe travel through this region.

In Alexandria, the second largest city in Egypt, located on the Mediterranean Sea North West of Delta, we rented a cab and toured the year-round resort. E. M. Forster once said that the best way of seeing Alexandria is to wander aimlessly about. We took his advice.

The city center stretches from Saad Zaghloul Square, to the seafront, there is a statue of Saad Pacha. This was formerly the site of the Caesareum, a magnificent temple built by Cleopatra and Marc Anthony. Two famous obelisks (one known as 'Cleoparta's Needle", now on the Embankment in London; the other in New York's Central Park) were once here but all traces of the temple have disappeared.

Not much of this did I remember from our visit to the surrounding area in 1984.

I think that it is true that one cannot go home again. Time changes everything, yet our hearts long to feel and our eyes yearn to see only what we want to remember.

The Negro Speaks of Rivers (1926)   Langston
Hughes
The Dry Salvages (1941) T. S. Eliot
The Discovery of the Future (1901) Herbert
George Wells
Ich grolle nicht   Heinrich Heine
King Lear   Shakespeare
Rock Me To Sleep (1860) Elizabeth Akers Allen
The Hold Bible Song of Solomon
Orbit (1973)   Robert Traill Spence Lowell
John Keats

Web Resources

www.touregypt.net
www.lonelyplanet.com
www.historyforkids.org
www.ancient.egypt.org